CELEBRATING HOLIDAYS

Hanukkah

by Rachel Grack

BLASTOFF!
2
READERS

BELLWETHER MEDIA • MINNEAPOLIS, MN

Note to Librarians, Teachers, and Parents:

Blastoff! Readers are carefully developed by literacy experts and combine standards-based content with developmentally appropriate text.

Level 1 provides the most support through repetition of high-frequency words, light text, predictable sentence patterns, and strong visual support.

Level 2 offers early readers a bit more challenge through varied simple sentences, increased text load, and less repetition of high-frequency words.

Level 3 advances early-fluent readers toward fluency through increased text and concept load, less reliance on visuals, longer sentences, and more literary language.

Level 4 builds reading stamina by providing more text per page, increased use of punctuation, greater variation in sentence patterns, and increasingly challenging vocabulary.

Level 5 encourages children to move from "learning to read" to "reading to learn" by providing even more text, varied writing styles, and less familiar topics.

Whichever book is right for your reader, Blastoff! Readers are the perfect books to build confidence and encourage a love of reading that will last a lifetime!

This edition first published in 2017 by Bellwether Media, Inc.

No part of this publication may be reproduced in whole or in part without written permission of the publisher. For information regarding permission, write to Bellwether Media, Inc., Attention: Permissions Department, 5357 Penn Avenue South, Minneapolis, MN 55419.

Library of Congress Cataloging-in-Publication Data

Names: Koestler-Grack, Rachel A., 1973- author.
Title: Hanukkah / by Rachel Grack.
Description: Minneapolis, MN : Bellwether Media, Inc., 2017. | Series: Blastoff! Readers: Celebrating Holidays | Includes bibliographical references and index. | Audience: Ages: 5-8. | Audience: Grades: K to Grade 3.
Identifiers: LCCN 2016034191 (print) | LCCN 2016035315 (ebook) | ISBN 9781626175952 (hardcover : alk. paper) | ISBN 9781681033259 (ebook)
Subjects: LCSH: Hanukkah–Juvenile literature.
Classification: LCC BM695.H3 K595 2017 (print) | LCC BM695.H3 (ebook) | DDC 296.4/35–dc23
LC record available at https://lccn.loc.gov/2016034191

Editor: Christina Leaf   Designer: Lois Stanfield

Printed in the United States of America, North Mankato, MN.

Table of Contents

Hanukkah Is Here!   4

What Is Hanukkah?   6

Who Celebrates Hanukkah?   8

Hanukkah Beginnings   10

Time to Celebrate   14

Hanukkah Traditions!   16

Glossary   22

To Learn More   23

Index   24

Hanukkah Is Here!

The winter sun has just set.
A family says a prayer.

Then, they light one candle of the **menorah**. Hanukkah has begun!

What Is Hanukkah?

Hanukkah is a **Jewish** holiday. Families light special candles during this **Festival** of Lights.

They sing **hymns** and give to **charity**.

Who Celebrates Hanukkah?

Jews celebrate Hanukkah. They remember their **ancestors**.

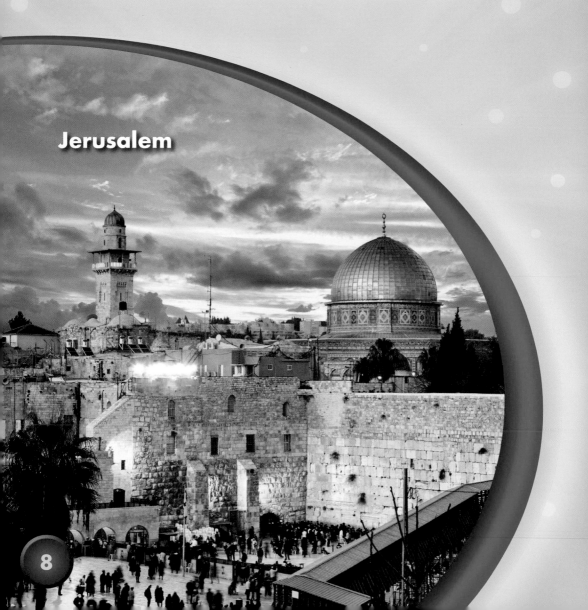

Jerusalem

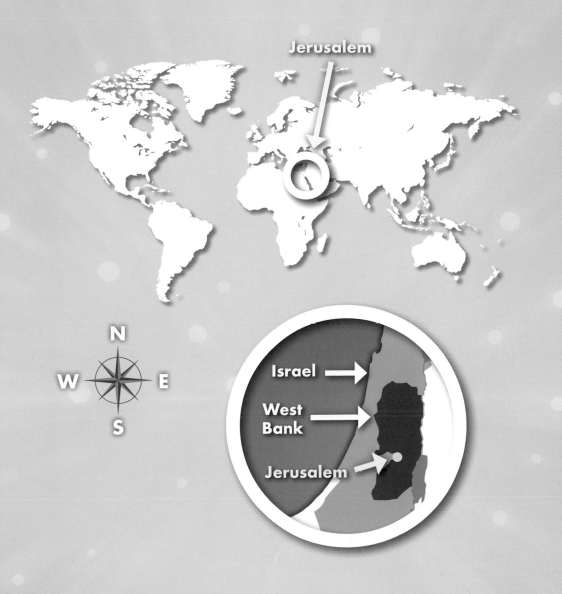

They honor when the Jews **dedicated** a new **temple** in Jerusalem.

9

Hanukkah Beginnings

site of the
Jewish Temple

Hanukkah began more than
2,000 years ago. The Greeks
controlled the Jewish temple.

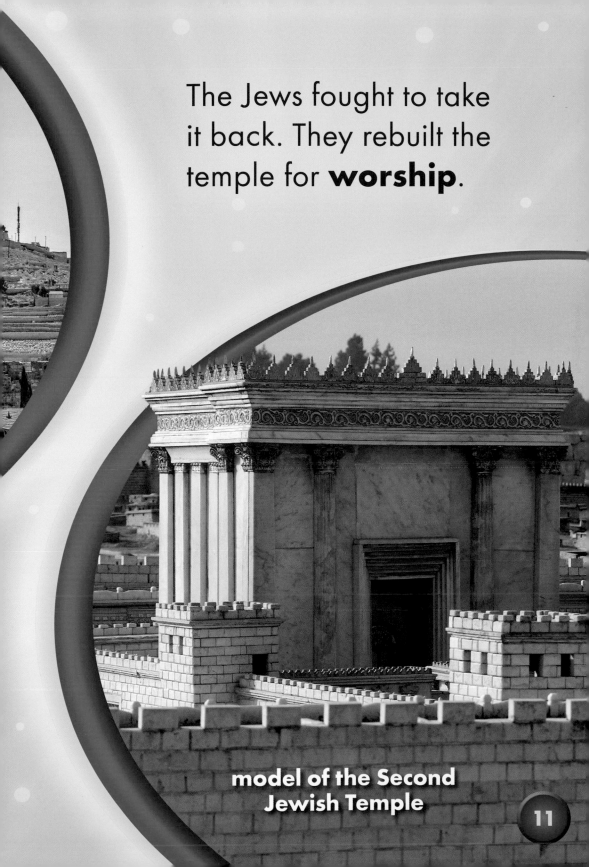

The Jews fought to take it back. They rebuilt the temple for **worship**.

model of the Second Jewish Temple

11

The story says that the Jews lit a lamp in the new temple. They only had enough oil for one night.

modern Jew lighting Hanukkah lamp

The lamp burned for eight days.
It was a **miracle**!

Hanukkah is usually in December. It follows the **Hebrew** calendar.

Word	Pronunciation
dreidel	DRAY-dell
Hanukkah	HA-nuk-kah
latkes	LAHT-kahs
menorah	meh-NOR-ah
sufganiyot	soof-geh-nee-OT

Hanukkah begins on day 25 of the month Kislev. It lasts for eight days.

People light eight candles in the menorah during Hanukkah.

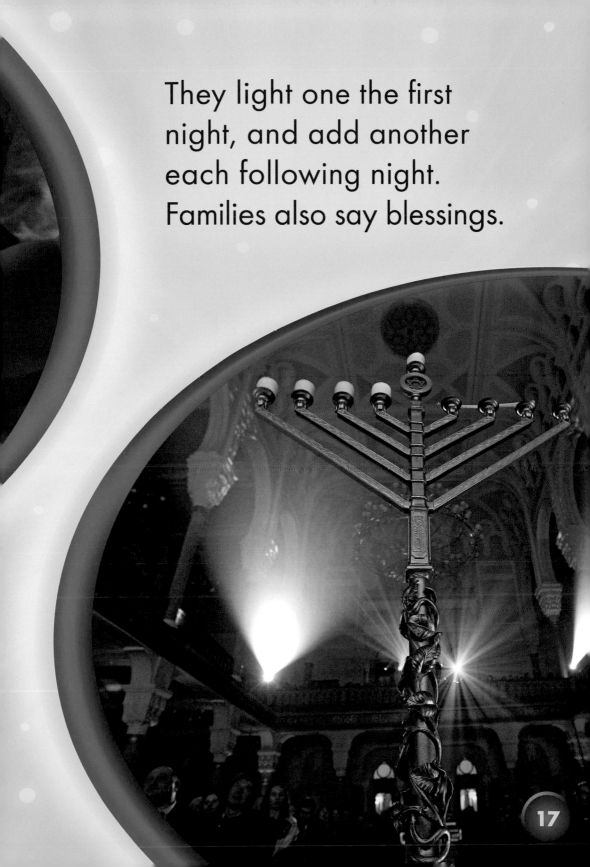

They light one the first night, and add another each following night. Families also say blessings.

17

Some children play the *dreidel* game for candy or coins. This dice-like top is marked with Hebrew letters. The markings stand for "A great miracle happened there."

Play Dreidel!

What You Need:

- a dreidel
- chocolate coins, ten for each player

What the Hebrew Letters Mean:

נ *Nun* means "nothing": Do nothing

ג *Gimel* means "everything": Take everything in the pot

ה *Hey* means "half": Take half the pot

ש *Shin* means "put in": Add a coin to the pot

What You Do:

1. Each player takes ten coins.
2. Sit in a circle.
3. Each player puts one coin in the center, or "pot."
4. Take turns spinning the dreidel.
5. See how the dreidel lands. Do what it says.
6. The last player with coins wins!

Many Hanukkah foods are made with oil. People remember the miracle of the lamp. They fry potato *latkes* and eat jelly donuts called *sufganiyot*.

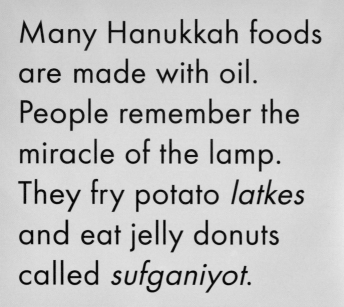

latkes

sufganiyot

Jewish families celebrate
their history!

Glossary

ancestors—relatives who lived long ago

charity—gifts to the poor or someone in need

dedicated—honored something new

festival—celebration

Hebrew—Jewish; Jews are also called Hebrews.

hymns—songs of worship and praise

Jewish—related to Judaism, a religion that began in Israel and teaches belief in one God

menorah—the Hebrew word for candlestick; a Hanukkah menorah, called a *hanukkiah*, has nine branches.

miracle—an unusual or wonderful event sometimes believed to be caused by God

temple—the Jewish place of worship

worship—the act of showing respect and love for a god

To Learn More

AT THE LIBRARY
Adler, David A. *The Story of Hanukkah*. New York, N.Y.: Holiday House, 2011.

Aloian, Molly. *Hanukkah*. New York, N.Y.: Crabtree Pub. Co., 2009.

Balsley, Tilda. *Maccabee!: The Story of Hanukkah*. Minneapolis, Minn.: Kar-Ben Pub., 2010.

ON THE WEB
Learning more about Hanukkah is as easy as 1, 2, 3.

1. Go to www.factsurfer.com.

2. Enter "Hanukkah" into the search box.

3. Click the "Surf" button and you will see a list of related web sites.

With factsurfer.com, finding more information is just a click away.

Index

ancestors, 8
blessings, 17
candle, 5, 6, 16, 17
charity, 7
dates, 14, 15
dreidel, 18, 19
family, 4, 6, 17, 21
Festival of Lights, 6
foods, 20
Greeks, 10
Hebrew, 14, 18, 19
hymns, 7
Jerusalem, 8, 9
Jews, 8, 9, 11, 12

lamp, 12, 13, 20
menorah, 5, 16
miracle, 13, 18, 20
oil, 12, 20
prayer, 4
pronunciation, 15
temple, 9, 10, 11, 12
winter, 4
worship, 11

The images in this book are reproduced through the courtesy of: D. Hurst/ Alamy, front cover; ASAP/ Alamy, pp. 4, 4-5; Noam Armonn, pp. 6-7; Kwame Zikomo/ Purestock/ SuperStock, p. 7; Sean Pavone/ Alamy, p. 8; OPIS Zagreb, pp. 10-11; Flik47, p. 11; Uriel Sinai/ Getty Images, p. 12; Philippe Lissac/ picture-alliance/ Godong/ Newscom, p. 13; Ira Berger/ Alamy, p. 14; Pavel Vakhrushev, p. 15; ChameleonsEye, pp. 16-17; ITAR-TASS Photo Agency/ Alamy, p. 17; National Geographic Creative/ Alamy, p. 18; Margie Hurwich, p. 19; TheCrimsonMonkey, p. 20 (left); irkaz, p. 20 (right); Noam Armonn/ Alamy, pp. 20-21; Tim Masters, p. 22.